John Thompson's
Easiest Piano Course

——•——

PART EIGHT

——•——

ISBN 978-0-87718-019-7

WILLIS MUSIC

EXCLUSIVELY DISTRIBUTED BY

HAL•LEONARD®
CORPORATION
7777 W. BLUEMOUND RD. P.O. BOX 13819
MILWAUKEE, WISCONSIN 53213

Visit Hal Leonard Online at
www.halleonard.com

FOREWORD

Part Eight presents material slightly more advanced than that found in Part Seven, and is designed to develop 'style' as well as technical fluency on the part of the pupil.

More demands on Musicianship also should be made throughout the progress of this book.

As a supplementary book of Technic, the author's THIRD GRADE VELOCITY is recommended.

Since each pupil is 'a law unto himself', no two pupils can be handled alike. Therefore the book is planned to allow the teacher a wide latitude.

The prime purpose of the book is to present **material** which can be adapted to the individual pupil's needs according to the discretion of the teacher.

John Thompson

CONTENTS

Play this with light, forearm attack and try to suggest the mysterious, dancing light of the Will o' the wisp. Note that the accents are wedge-shaped. This indicates more emphasis than that given the usual accent sign.

Etude
Will O' The Wisp

FRANZ BEHR

In all dance forms, rhythm is uppermost. In addition to the normal accent, note the sostenuto sign ($\bar{p}$) over the first note of each measure in the right hand. All slurs should be tossed off rather sharply. Give a rather vigorous treatment throughout to suggest the clumping of the heavy wooden shoes.

Clog Dance

The Time Signature of this piece is Three-Eight — which means three counts to each measure and one count to each eighth note. This is a study in playing forearm staccato in one hand against finger legato in the other. After it has been learned in slow tempo, try to build up the speed, with accuracy of course!

Etude

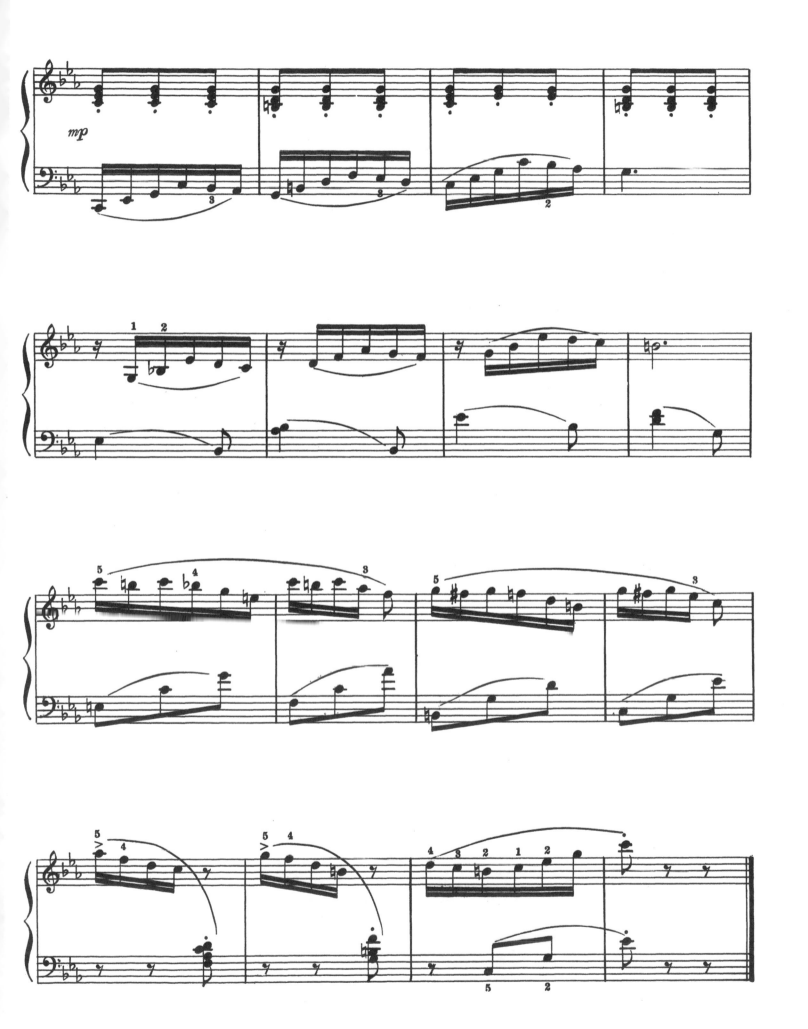

This piece was written as a tribute to the beautiful city of Pest, which forms half of the twin cities known as Budapest, capital of Hungary. The two cities are separated by the river Danube. The original version of this number presents the melody in octaves and it is very popular as a four-handed piece. Keep a well marked rhythm throughout and make sharp contrast between staccato and legato.

from
Salut á Pest

Henri Kowalski
(Arr.)

Here is a study in smooth finger legato alternating with two and three-note slurs. Play it with all the care given to a solo piece. It contains pianistic passages that will occur in many of your future pieces.

Etude

BURGMÜLLER

Johann Nepomuk Hummel was a celebrated pianist and composer of his day. His compositions are distinguished for excellence of construction and brilliancy of ornament. He was born in Pressburg, Germany in 1778 and died in Weimar in 1837.

Scherzo means a joke or jest. When applied as a title, it means an instrumental composition in humorous character. This should give you a clue as to the proper interpretation of the following number.

from

Scherzo

J. N. HUMMEL
1778-1837

THE DOUBLE SHARP

This example presents a new Accidental — the *Double Sharp*. It looks like this ✕ and is used to indicate that the following note be raised *two half-steps*.

Mazurka

ERIK MEYER-HELMUND
1861-1932

Allegro, ma non troppo

Fine

18

The following is a study in arpeggio playing and consists of broken chords divided between the hands. The transfer from one hand to the other must be made as smoothly as possible. Each group should be played with a rolling motion of the hand, using the minimum amount of finger action.

Etude

BURGMÜLLER

Arcangelo Corelli was one of the very early Italian musicians and was recognized in his day as a great violinist and composer. Very little is known of his life until he settled in Rome at the age of 28, where he enjoyed the friendship and patronage of Cardinal Ottoboni, a lover of the arts in general and of music especially.

Corelli made friends with many famous painters and his chief hobby was that of collecting valuable pictures.

His greatest work was the Concerti-grossi which was published only six weeks before his death.

He was buried in the Pantheon at Rome not far from the tomb of the famous painter, Raphael. Cardinal Ottoboni errected a handsome monument to his memory and a statue of him was placed in the Vatican.

It is claimed he laid a firm foundation for future violin technic and that his works advanced materially, the progress of musical composition.

A GIGUE is an old Italian dance, played in lively tempo and it was often used as the last movement of a Suite. It is thought that the name derived from the GIGA, which was an early Italian fiddle.

In the following example, be sure to make sharp contrast between staccato and legato and toss off all slurs crisply.

Try to create an atmosphere of mirth and gaiety suggesting the dancing of happy peasants.

Preserve strict tempo and well-defined rhythm at all times.

from
Gigue

ARCANGELO CORELLI
1653-1713

This piece should be played with all the smoothness and grace associated with the dancers of the ballet. As the figures pass from one hand to the other, the transfer should be made without perceptible break. This is a piece that can be used for recital purposes.

Air de Ballet

JOHN THOMPSON

Here is an etude in finger dexterity. Practice it carefully as it will help to improve your technic. The arpeggio figure on the last line should sound as smoothly as though played with one hand.

Etude

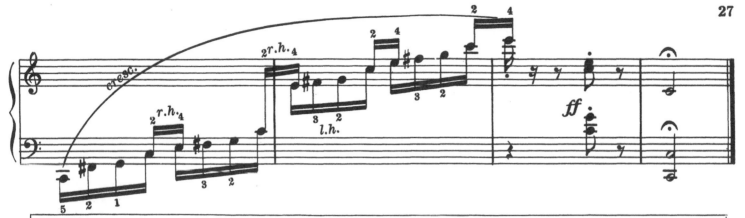

This theme from the great Brahms Symphony should have the effect of a big Chorale. Play the chords with sustained forearm strokes and allow the weight of the hand to rest on the upper notes of the right hand so as to give more resonance to the melody tones.

from
Symphony No. 1

JOHANNES BRAHMS

This is a piano arrangement of one of Mendelssohn's most beautiful songs. Play the melody with your best singing tone, but because of the low register, try not to let it sound "too thick".
See if you can imitate the beautiful quality of a cello.

from
On Wings of Song

FELIX MENDELSSOHN

Here is a study in bouncing wrist staccato. Perform it in the style of a Scherzo — light and playful.

Etude

Zdenko Fibich was born in Seborsitz, Bohemia, in 1850 and died in Prague in 1900. As a composer, he was one of the foremost in the young Czech group.

He wrote three symphonies, several Operas and a number of Symphonic Poems for orchestra. The excerpt presented here has been made extremely popular in America by means of the radio. Play it with utmost expression.

Poem

ZDENKO FIBICH
(Arr.)

Here is a waltz that should be played in light, care-free manner with good style and rhythmical 'snap'. It should make a good recital number as it has the quality of sounding much more difficult than it really is.

Valse

Franz Drdla was born in Saar, Moravia in 1868. He made successful concert tours as a violinist in Europe, lived for a time in the United States, then returned to Prague and Vienna. One of the most popular of his violin pieces is the SOUVENIR, arranged here as a piano solo.

Souvenir

FRANZ DRDLA
(Arr.)

This is a study in contrasting staccato and legato. Keep a sharp rhythm at all times and let the staccato notes be very 'pointed'.

Etude

Tritsch Tratsch Polka

JOHANN STRAUSS

Barcarolle means Boat Song. Be sure to observe the left hand slurs which, when properly applied, give the effect of a rocking motion in imitation of the gondolas as they glide over the inland canals of Venice.

Barcarolle

Certificate of Merit

This certifies that

....

has successfully completed

BOOK EIGHT

of

JOHN THOMPSON'S

"EASIEST PIANO COURSE"

and is eligible for promotion to

JOHN THOMPSON'S

FOURTH GRADE RED BOOK

of

The Modern Course for the Piano

....
Teacher

Date...